U.S. COAST GUARD

JEN BESEL

BLACK RABBIT BOOKS

Bolt Jr. is published by Black Rabbit Books
P.O. Box 227, Mankato, Minnesota, 56002
www.blackrabbitbooks.com

Michael Sellner, designer and photo researcher

Names: Besel, Jennifer M., author.
Title: U.S. Coast Guard / by Jen Besel.
Other titles: United States Coast Guard
Description: Mankato, Minnesota : Black Rabbit Books, [2023] | Series: Bolt Jr. mighty military | Includes bibliographical references and index. | Audience: Ages 6-8 | Audience: Grades K-1 | Summary: "Engage young readers with information about the U.S. Coast Guard. From the group's fleet of boats to the people who drive them, readers will learn all about how the U.S. Coast Guard protects the United States"– Provided by publisher.
Identifiers: LCCN 2021022165 (print) | LCCN 2021022166 (ebook) | ISBN 9781623107628 (hardcover) | ISBN 9781644665893 (paperback) | ISBN 9781623107680 (ebook)
Subjects: LCSH: United States. Coast Guard–Juvenile literature.
Classification: LCC VG53 .B46 2023 (print) | LCC VG53 (ebook) | DDC 363.28/60973–dc23
LC record available at https://lccn.loc.gov/2021022165
LC ebook record available at https://lccn.loc.gov/2021022166

Image Credits

Alamy: AB Forces News Collection, 11, 18; APFootage, 23; Pete Titmuss, 20–21; Terrance Klassen, 13; US Coast Guard Photo, 8–9; Warships, 6–7; AP Images: DAVID J. PHILLIP, 4–5; Dreamstime: Dpecheux, 10; Eholmes5, 15; Getty: Handout, 12; Shutterstock: Dzmitry Kim, 2, 24; Eliks, 4; Francois Poirier, 14; objectsforall, 21; U.S. Department of Defense: Coast Guard Petty Officer 1st Class Bret Fogle, 1; U.S. Department of Homeland Security: United States Coast Guard, Cover

Contents

CHAPTER 1

What Is the U.S. Coast Guard?

A helicopter flies above a **flooded** city. People are stuck on a house below. A Coast Guard member gets lowered down. She helps lift the people to safety.

flooded: covered with water

U.S.
COAST GUA
6011

On the Water

The Coast Guard is part of the U.S. military. This group does water rescues. Members clean up oceans and rivers. They also stop attacks.

COMPARING COAST GUARD WATERCRAFT

boats

less than 65 feet (20 meters) long
often used near shore
can be attached to cutters

cutters

more than 65 feet (20 m) long

use spy equipment

members can live on it

EXPLORING A Cutter

can carry helicopters
S. COAST GUARD
can break through icy water

CHAPTER 2

Training

All members start with **basic training**. They learn to use weapons. They build their muscles. They also study rules.

basic training: the first few weeks of learning for someone who has joined the military

FACT

They learn how to fight fires too.

U.S. COAST GUARD

On the Job

After training, members go on to jobs. Some catch people breaking laws. Others study **icebergs**. Some help sick animals.

iceberg: a large floating piece of ice

U.S. Coast Guard Bases and Stations

KEY

= U.S. Coast Guard bases and boat stations

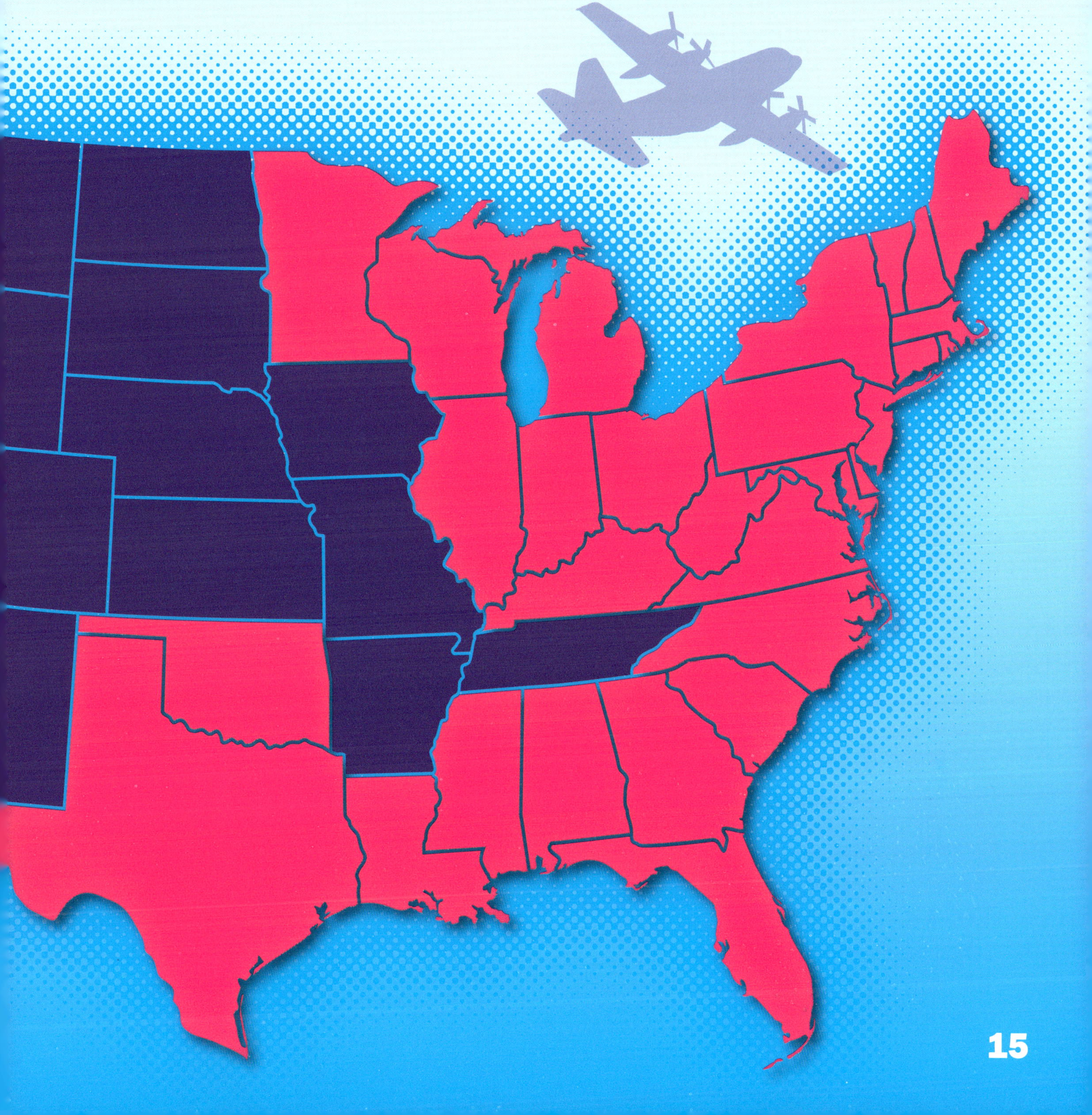

CHAPTER 3

Gear and Weapons

The Coast Guard uses many ships. Members use cutters for rescues. Icebreakers carry scientists. They do experiments.

FACT

Some boats have machine guns.

U. S. COAST GUARD

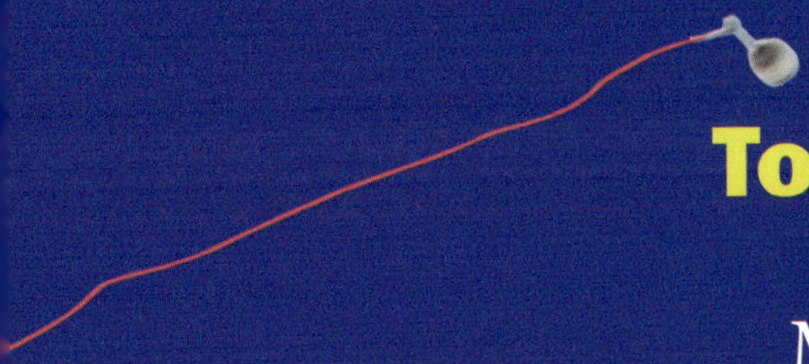

To the Rescue

Members use line guns to help boats. The guns shoot ropes to the boats. Members then drag the boats to safety.

Distance a Line Gun Can Throw

about 850 feet (259 m)

Bonus Facts

The Coast Guard started in 1790.

It has about 42,000 members.

Members also help lost hikers.

Members care for more than 100,000 miles (160,934 kilometers) of **coastline**.

coastline: the land along the edge of a body of water

READ MORE/WEBSITES

Billings, Tanner. *The U.S. Coast Guard.* Inside the U.S. Military. New York: Rosen Publishing, 2022.

Miller, Marie-Therese. *The U.S. Coast Guard in Action.* U.S. Military Branches. Minneapolis: Lerner Publications, 2023.

Nagle, Frances. *Coast Guard Boats to the Rescue!* Rescue Riders. New York: Gareth Stevens Publishing, 2023.

United States Coast Guard
www.uscg.mil/

U.S. Coast Guard—YouTube Channel
www.youtube.com/user/USCGImargery

HAND
HOLD
USCG
U.S. COAST GUARD

GLOSSARY

basic training (BAY-sik TRAYN-ing)—the first few weeks of learning for someone who has joined the military

coastline (KOHST-lahyn)—the land along the edge of a body of water

flooded (FLUH-ded)—covered with water

iceberg (IYS-burg)—a large floating piece of ice

INDEX